A MYSTIC DREAM OF 4

A sonnet sequence based on the life of
William Rowan Hamilton

IGGY McGOVERN

ACKNOWLEDGEMENTS

The author is grateful to the following for financial
support of the publication of this work:

TCD Association & Trust
TCD School of Physics
Dublin Institute of Advanced Studies
Poetry Ireland

Thanks are also due to La Fondation Irlandaise
for the provision of a residency at
Centre Culturel Irlandais in Paris.

'My Best Girl', poem by Eamon de Valera.
By permission of the de Valera family and The
National Library of Ireland

"The quaternion [was] born, as a curious offspring of a quaternion of parents, say of geometry, algebra, metaphysics, and poetry."

— *William Rowan Hamilton*

Contents

PART III 1835 – 1850 METAPHYSICS

PART IV 1850 – 1865 POETRY

Preface

WILLIAM ROWAN HAMILTON was born in 1805, the only son of Archibald and Sarah Hamilton of Dominick Street in Dublin. As a consequence of his father's bankruptcy he was sent to live with his uncle in Trim in 1808, and remained there until he entered Trinity College in 1823. Four years later, while still in the final year of his degree, he was appointed to the Andrews Chair of Astronomy of Dublin University. He was knighted in 1835 and died in 1865.

That brief biography skims the surface of a multilayered life. Hamilton became the foremost mathematician of his day, a brilliant mind that was informed by a passionate nature, as well as by 'a taste for verse'. In the former regard, his lifelong feelings for his first love Catherine Disney, despite their separate marriages, were just within the bounds of Victorian respectability and occasioned attempts at self-harm on either side; in the latter regard, he was a close friend of Wordsworth, to whom he sent his poems.

This suggests that Hamilton's life might be a fit topic for a sequence of poems, specifically a sequence of sonnets, a form much used by Hamilton. Although Hamilton preferred the Petrarchan form, the more narrative-friendly Shakespearean form is used here. Moreover, the number four insists on recognition, reflecting his discovery of quaternions, four-membered numbers that today underpin spacecraft manipulation and cartoon character tumbling. The number of sonnets in the sequence is equal to the cube of four, and the title *A Mystic Dream of 4* is from a line in one of Hamilton's own sonnets.

Like any book of poetry this is a work of imagination. It purports to tell the story of Hamilton's life, but with a degree of poetic license. The narrative is provided by 64 'talking heads', mainly individuals who knew Hamilton personally. These include family relatives, scientific colleagues, poets and other friends. As might be expected, many of these are more interested in talking about themselves, but they still take the narrative forward.

Hamilton's 60 years are roughly divided into 4 sections with 16 sonnets per section. The four sections are given headings that derive from Hamilton's statement — the book's epigraph — that quaternions had four parents, namely, geometry, algebra, metaphysics and poetry; moreover, the first sonnet in each section is in the voice of one of these four 'parents'.

The eponymous sonnet of each section is followed by 14 person-sonnets. With two exceptions these are persons who were known to Hamilton. However, Hamilton's mathematical legacy has continued into the present time, and with strong historical resonances in Ireland. Thus, the penultimate two sonnets of the final section feature two people who were born long after Hamilton's death, namely, Eamon de Valera and Erwin Schrödinger. De Valera was a devotee of Hamilton's quaternion algebra; he was also instrumental in bringing Schrödinger to Dublin and the famous Schrödinger Equation contains the Hamiltonian function. Other significant discoveries by Hamilton are referred to elsewhere in the sequence, notably the prediction of conical refraction.

There are two significant absences from the sequence. The first is Catherine Disney, the woman with whom Hamilton fell in love as a student; the dramatic intersections of her life with that of Hamilton's are better told by others, notably her brothers and her husband.

And, of course, Hamilton himself gets no right of reply. That being so, Hamilton is referred to throughout the sonnets in the third person, and that nomenclature (he, him, his etc) is reserved for Hamilton *alone*.

Which leaves the matter of the last sonnet in each section. Hamilton lived in a time of major upheaval in Ireland, both religious and political. However, the historical event that looms largest is The Great Famine. For this and other narrative reasons, it has seemed appropriate to leave the task of closure to the supreme ironist, Death.

Finally, acknowledgements are due to the authors of two key texts. First and foremost is the monumental 3-volume work *Life of Sir William Rowan Hamilton* by his contemporary Robert Percival Graves, published by Dublin University Press in 1882; this, as the subtitle promises, contains 'poems, correspondence and miscellaneous writings' – Hamilton was a compulsive letter-writer and his collected correspondence is an invaluable source. But Graves was not mathematically inclined and this side of the story is more comprehensively told in the recent *Sir William Rowan Hamilton* by Thomas L. Hankins, published by The Johns Hopkins University Press in 1980.

— Iggy McGovern
Dublin 2013

Timeline

1805	Birth of WRH
1808	Sent to Trim
1814	Death of Aunt Sydney
1817	Death of mother
1818	Contest with Zerah Colburn
1819	Death of father
1820	Meets future College Tutor
1823	First placed in TCD Entrance Examination
1824	Meets novelist Maria Edgeworth
	'On Caustics' submitted to Royal Irish Academy
	Meets Catherine Disney
1825	Catherine marries Reverend Barlow
	'On Caustics' rejected by Royal Irish Academy
1827	Publication of 'Theory of System of Rays'
	Appointed Andrews Professor of Astronomy
	Meets Wordsworth
	Takes up residence at Dunsink Observatory
1830	Meets Catherine in Armagh
1831	Meets Ellen and Aubrey DeVere
1832	Prediction of conical refraction
1833	Marries Helen Bayly
1834	Publication of 'On a General Method in Dynamics'
1835	Knighted by Lord Lieutenant
1837	Elected President of RIA
	Publication of 'Algebra as the Science of Pure Time'
1843	Discovery of quaternions
1845	Catherine visits Dunsink
1847	Deaths of Uncle James and James MacCullagh
1848	Catherine attempts suicide
	Smith O'Brien Rebellion
1851	Death of Eliza

PART I

1805 – 1820

Geometry

GEOMETRY

Once, any pupil could define me best:
"points, lines, angles and figures", could amuse
The table with the Christmas cracker jest
About 'the squaw' on the hypotenuse!

I was the Lord of Space, the one in three
Dimensions where you lived each mortal day,
Coordinates describing pointedly
A final resting place in graveyard clay.

But that's to come; for now reserve your pity,
Observe the longitude and latitude
Of Dominick Street, the kingdom's second city,
A multigravida in plenitude

And my coy mistress, Time, deploys her power
To act precisely on the midnight hour.

Hamilton was reputedly born at midnight, a popular token of
greatness. It has been suggested that, had he lived longer, he
would have anticipated Einstein's concept of space-time.

ARCHIBALD ROWAN (Godparent)

Who fears to speak of '98? Not I!
I did my bit, converting Killyleagh.
They said I got off light — no gallows high;
I tricked my gaolers, hence my odyssey

Through France, America and Germany,
Eleven years of hand-to-mouth exile
But then, thanks to The Crown's short memory,
Recalled to life back in my Emerald Isle.

O, what a night! Great bonfires lit the sky,
Whereafter many heads were slow to mend.
Young Hamilton did well — I can't think why
They took so hard against me at the end ...

The boy? Ah yes! You know he bears my name?
In that, at least, he'll have his share of fame!

Archibald Rowan was a United Irishman who was forced to
live in exile for many years after the 1798 rebellion.
Hamilton's father acted for him in his absence. Hamilton was
given the Rowan name after his godparent.

ARCHIBALD HAMILTON (Father)

No, not a year I'm likely to forget,
1805, and old man Rowan dead;
I had The Volunteers aid and abet
Eviction of the floozy from that bed.

And all the while petitioning The Crown
To let the heir return to Killyleagh,
No effort in portrayal of a clown
Unlikely to offend in any way.

In fact, that business kept me from our door
When my dear Sarah came into her time;
Relief then, after all that went before,
The baby's cry meshed with the Christchurch chime.

A welcome brother for our darling Grace;
At last, another man about the place.

Hamilton's father worked to secure the return of Archibald
Rowan to claim his inheritance. This included the effective
pardon for his earlier rebel activity and the dislodgement of the
mistress of Rowan's father. Hamilton's mother had at least one
miscarriage prior to his birth.

SARAH HUTTON HAMILTON (Mother)

We Huttons were above the hoi polloi,
Coachmakers, solid citizens of worth.
Well matched with the apothecary's boy,
I thought to make our mark upon this earth.

My poor dear husband, always a good word
For everyone, too easily deceived:
Not least that rebel-rousing, preening bird —
I will not mince my words — the blackguard thieved

And left us in our present parlous state
Of bankruptcy, privation, coals of shame;
Morality is scarce among the great.
I will not have the mention of the name

That for my children, while I had their bearing,
Ensured our relatives must have their rearing.

Archibald Rowan welshed on the debts incurred on his behalf by Hamilton's father, driving the latter into bankruptcy. As a consequence the children were farmed out to relations. Accordingly, the Rowan was dropped from Hamilton's name but he re-adopted it as a young man.

REVEREND JAMES HAMILTON (Uncle)

Curate of Trim, my first and final station,
A College man, The Classics; Cicero writes
"A happy life consists in — my translation —
Tranquility of mind"; these were my lights.

I taught a small schoolhouse with little fuss,
From *mensa* to the seventeen times table,
Until my nephew came to board with us,
My brother's situation far from stable.

Their loss our gain, as all of us could tell:
A three year old savant, whose tiny mind
Was like a five mile deep artesian well
In which to pour the wisdom of mankind.

My interest at once compound and simple
Like finding The Child Saviour in The Temple.

Hamilton lodged with his Uncle James from the age of three until he entered Trinity College. From James he inherited a love of The Classics, an interest in foreign languages and an inclination to conservative politics and religion; his eventual forays into mathematics did not entirely please his teacher and effective guardian.

ELIZABETH HAMILTON (Aunt by marriage)

There never was the beat of him, I say:
So quick and his recall sharp as a bell
And quite untroubled by my husband's way
Of teaching little children how to spell.

They start with words of just one syllable
In which the letter *a* is to be found;
When these have been learned off, well, then they will
Move on to those with *b*, and, I'll be bound,

Go all the way to *z* but, Heavens, then
It's back to *a*, this time for words of two
And round and round and round they go again:
Too much, I fear — but that's 'twixt me and you.

Such words not found in our vocabulary;
You'd swear he'd swallowed Johnson's Dictionary!

Hamilton's uncle held unusual views about the teaching of
language; his wife was a more conventional tutor.

SYDNEY HAMILTON (Aunt)

A privilege to be his pedagogue
In Computation, Hebrew, Latin, Greek …
He wears his learning lightly, the sweet rogue,
So easy got and fashioned into cheek,

As when my call to rising he negates,
Protesting, with no want of winning guile,
That since Aurora'd scarce unbarred her gates
He might, if it would please, lie on a while.

Regarding then his bath on Saturday,
He must refuse, he says, on pain of Hell
For, since he's learning Hebrew, he would pray
My leave to keep *their* Sabbath Day as well.

Our James will not allow him stray too far
Lest he be thought quite rude, if not bizarre!

Hamilton's paternal aunt also contributed to the school curriculum; her reports to Hamilton's father are testament to a considerable degree of precociousness in the child.

REVEREND RICHARD BUTLER (Vicar of Trim)

My curate is, no doubt, a clever man,
A dozen foreign tongues in easy reach
But not to be enrolled with those that can
Must stand with those that cannot, and so teach.

The nephew though is cut from different cloth:
Though barely into breeches, he can clown
As well as any adult, faith and troth,
He read us Greek, the book held upside down.

And caused no small amount of consternation
To Mrs Fox, declining her invite
To stay at Foxbrook with the observation
That *Mister Goosey* would not last the night!

Why, even Hamilton was fit to burst.
Perhaps then, on that showing, not the worst.

Mrs Goosey was a childen's book character; Hamilton evidently had wit well beyond his years. Reverend Butler had a significant influence on Hamilton's early social life, including an introduction to Maria Edgeworth.

GRACE HAMILTON (Sister)

Our parents left him in my daily care
When we were family in Dominick Street,
Before the aggravation and despair
When each must seek a separate retreat.

He went to board with Uncle James in Trim,
I and Eliza to my mother's people
In Manchester, so proper and so prim
beneath their strict Moravian squat steeple.

Restored to Trim, Eliza left behind
Our days were madcap, chasing after sheep,
Playacting Homer … yet I was not blind;
She was his soulmate, prayerful and deep.

The practical-poetical divide,
My Martha to her Mary must abide.

After her mother's early death Hamilton's older sister Grace took
on that role within the family. She subsequently organised
Hamilton's household at Dunsink Observatory until her brother's
marriage.

ELIZA HAMILTON (Sister)

So close in age we might be counted twin
Though kept apart for much of our young years
— and there are some who think it is no sin
To strike a twin to seek the other's tears?

Of course, there was no similar connection
Yet I would venture some telepathy
Conveyed a brother-sisterly affection
Across the ether of our empathy.

We differed only in our core belief,
In which regard I constantly shall strive
To bring him joy before that sure relief
When we shall be as *Mark 12:25*

"Wherein they neither marry, nor are given
In marriage but are as angels in heaven"

Eliza, a close confidante of Hamilton, was a poet and a
pietist; their letters contain endearments that seem strange to
the modern reader. She kept a record of the seminal
discussion between Hamilton and Wordsworth on the
relative merits of science and poetry, during the latter's visit
to Dunsink.

SYDNEY HAMILTON (Sister)

I do recall, it was the second year
After our mother's death, or not much later:
We're all out on Cross Avenue to cheer
My brother riding his *Accelerator.*

He seemed to have no end of energy;
He'd swim as strongly as the great grey seal
And then stride off to town to watch a play
— I thought him half in love with Miss O'Neill.

Such larks we had, as when he organized
The Honourable Society of Four:
The letter to 'The King' that we devised
Petitioning to keep him one week more.

In hindsight, time was not in long supply;
The royal barge was slowly passing by.

The *Accelerator* was an early form of bicycle; Elizabeth O'Neill
was a famous actress, later Lady Becher; 'The King' was
Hamilton's father. The Honourable Society of Four seems
prefigurative of quaternions. Sydney was the most scientifically
inclined of Hamilton's sisters, contributing to the astronomical
work at Dunsink Observatory.

ARCHIANNA HAMILTON (Sister)

I have to say this makes a pleasant change:
A canvass of *my* view on anything.
You'd think I was afflicted with the mange
Or some such other, what's-its-name, wormring?

I do at times get some words back to front
And must endure my sisters' huff and puff
But nobody is perfect — to be blunt,
One genius in the family is enough.

In all those letters back and forth I may
Get mention thrice, like *in memoriam*.
Runt of the litter, I make bold to say
Am I not great to be just as I am?

Would it have harmed a single thing alive
To make it a society of five?

Archianna, Hamilton's youngest sister, rarely features in the
Hamilton family correspondence, suggesting that she may have
had a mild disability; she died relatively young.

ZERAH COLBURN (Performer)

How many minutes since Christ went to Heaven?
What are the two prime factors of, say, four,
Two nine four, nine six seven, two nine seven?
All ere the second's hand will mark a score.

They billed me as *The Calculating Boy*.
What cogs and wheels were whirring 'neath my crown
To entertain street trader and Viceroy?
I almost met my match in that drab town …

I cared naught if I never understood
Exactly how I did it, whereas he
Was interested less in magnitude
And more in finding methodology.

I see him living well into his pension,
Computing Christ's velocity of Ascension!

Hamilton exhibited an early talent for mental arithmetic; he
competed with the American Zerah Colburn (and lost); his more
obstruse calculations included estimates of the volume of the
Temple of Edfu on the Nile and of the velocity of The Ascension.

THOMAS (TOMMY) FITZPATRICK (Schoolfriend)

The salad days: he left us far behind
In every subject, often knowing more
Than any teacher yet with no unkind
Put-down, the merest hint he knew the score.

Outside of class a cut above the rest;
He'd hold his own with fellows twice his age;
In sophistry impossible to best,
Bound either for The Commons or the stage.

The telegraph was one of his great tricks:
We 'talked' from Steeple Hill to Fairy Mount,
Each letter in a five by five matrix
Became a couplet of five signs of count,

With such success the village boys would run
From seeming agents of The Evil One!

Hamilton was a natural leader and he used the structure of The
Honourable Society of Four to organize his schoolfellows into a
senate. The 26th letter *w* was telegraphed as double-u.

MIRZA ABDUL HASSAN KHAN (Diplomat)

'Accept, illustrious visitant from Irann
(in Persian — this is just a rough translation)
A humble verse from one not yet a man
In awe of that proud culture of your nation ... '

And plenty more besides in much like vein,
Though no mistakes at all, the writing neat
But I was indisposed, a bad migraine
And so it was we never chanced to meet.

I had confused him with an older hand
Who'd demonstrated a much weaker grip;
I think a father urged him to this stand,
Convinced the son was bound for statesmanship.

Meanwhile, I keep within Bilton's Hotel
I tire of playing their tame infidel!

Young Hamilton wrote seeking an interview with the visiting
diplomat. He had a good command of many languages, including
Persian. His father thought he should aim for a position in the
Foreign Service. The spelling of Iran is as in the original letter.

DEATH

You did not think to meet me at this stage,
The ever-present uninvited guest,
But, whether of disease or plain old age,
I brought him news of three gone to their rest.

A mother's love's a blessing, that's the lore
Her leaving unremarked — was she surpassed
By surrogate Aunt Sydney, gone before,
The old girl spouting Latin to the last?

To lose *three* parents … ? let's not get ahead.
Here is the font of fatherly advice
In tip-top form and recently re-wed
Unlucky in the rolling of the dice.

He measures Mount Jerome's grey endless sky.
His fourteen years are told he may not cry.

PART II

1820 – 1835

Algebra

ALGEBRA

Did his 'illustrious visitant' know I
Can trace my roots — no pun! — back to that nation?
Al-jabr of Musa al-Khwarizmi,
Which means, I'm told, in that tongue 'restoration'

Though some, of course, would look beyond the word
To give the precedence to Diophantos,
Who'd deemed the negatives to be absurd
And on whose book did one John Chortasmenos

A thousand years on write this tart rebuff:
Your soul — I paraphrase — *be damned in Hell*
Because your theorems are just too damned tough!
and Fermat scribbled one last tease, as well.

Let no such mockery dilute the glory
Of his stout contributions to my story.

The proof of Fermat's infamous 'last theorem' (1637) was finally
given in 1995.

ARTHUR HAMILTON (Cousin)

When my first cousin, Archibald, died young
Our house became the children's home in town,
The boy with one foot on the bottom rung
Of that tall ladder leading to renown.

I like to think I did right, and I hope
That we were more as friends than father-son;
I bought him his first decent telescope,
Which he repaid in letters charged with pun

And rhyme, the stars observed, sharp depositions
Of all the lively goings-on in Trim.
At breakfast time we'd argue propositions
But I was much too slow to follow him.

You know he found an error by Laplace?
A book in French! Now that's what I call class.

Arthur's commitment to his young cousin included waiting
outside Trinity College for the announcement of the first year
examinations results. At the distant cry of "both premiums!"
Arthur exclaimed "I am at home – none could have both but
himself!"

DR THOMAS ELRINGTON (TCD Fellow)

Well, not to beat about the bush, I'll own
I never met his like in my born days,
A classicist, a perfect grecophone
While something of a dabbler in light-rays.

And from the point of his first entering
He came top of the section of his peers;
His *optime* for Homer answering
The first I'd given in some twenty years.

Thereafter, an unbroken string of Firsts
Except once when he seemed to fall apart,
Another one of Kennedy's outbursts
Or possibly some troubles of the heart?

His *optime* in Science at the last
Has nailed his colours firmly to that mast.

The College awarded 'premiums' in Science and in Classics in the form of credit at the university bookstore; formal examination grades ranged from *valde bene* to *vix medi*. An *optime* meant that the student had complete mastery of the subject. Apart from his difficult 2nd year (and Dr Kennedy's reputation for impossible examination questions) Hamilton's record was a series of *valde in omnius*.

MARIA EDGEWORTH (Author & Friend)

I think he came here first in '24,
The long vacation, and my father dead
Some seven years; it seemed to me he bore
A close resemblance to that noble head.

A second Newton! Doctor Brinkley says;
A man of Science, and The Arts to boot.
His conversation cheered our winter days
While Reverend Butler quietly made suit

To Harriet – I wish them happy lives!
Indeed, there was no lack of choice to hand
For my dear father had, in all, four wives
And fathered only girls, to beat the band.

I thought young Isaac might engage another
But he had eyes elsewhere, much to his bother.

Maria Edgeworth's extended family comprised a large number of sisters and half-sisters. The Newton label is fully justified in scientific terms but Hamilton's was the more likeable personality.

EDWARD DISNEY (Brother of Catherine)

We were best friends, as College students are
Yet I was blind to his infatuation
With Catherine, my sister, that her star
Was the bright nova in his constellation.

And he was unaware that she was meant
For old man Barlow, an unlikely lover,
A blow, it seemed, of murderous intent
From which he never really would recover.

And Catherine felt likewise, it appears,
With feelings that could not be undermined;
She did her duty, after floods of tears,
My father never one for change of mind

And nor was he, apparently unable
To choose another filly from our stable.

This was no mere student romance. Hamilton retained his
obsession with Catherine Disney throughout his life.

DRS McDONNELL, HARTE & LARDNER (MRIA)

They call us, behind backs, The Three Wise Men,
Our expertise acknowledged near and far,
Who showed with just a few strokes of the pen
We were unfit to follow yonder star.

On Caustics came, it seemed, out of the blue,
The author still in freshman college pants,
Soliciting our learnéd body's view
As to its scientific relevance.

We deemed it "novel", "highly interesting",
"considerable analytical skill",
Reserving to the end the scorpion sting
"abstract", "some reasoning eludes us still".

We could not understand the half of it
And hence were bound to let the young hare sit.

The rejection by the three members of the Royal Irish Academy
(MRIA) of Hamilton's first scientific paper was a further blow in
a very difficult year; it was subsequently published after some
revision. Hamilton's mode of expression was not always clear and
the decision to reject was probably the correct one.

CHARLES BOYTON (College Tutor)

A poor beginning to my Fellowship
That someone from a rural institution
— and soon to be my pupil! — should first pip
Me in a mathematical solution.

Thereafter, it was always far from clear
Who was the teacher and who was the taught
And, bar that wobble in his second year,
He deftly scooped the academic pot.

When old man Brinkley got the bishopric
I noised his name abroad, I hope with tact,
Defused the opposition — no small trick —
And gave The Board "one creditable act".

And if I puffed his astral appetite,
Well, look how History has proved me right!

Boyton did not hold his humiliation against his pupil and
worked to secure for Hamilton the Andrews Chair of
Astronomy, including an exaggeration of his talent as an
observer. The position, which included the post of Royal
Astronomer, became vacant when Brinkley was appointed
Bishop of Cloyne.

PROFESSOR JOHN BRINKLEY (Royal Astronomer)

At Board I had opposed his nomination
And argued that he had not really made
Much headway in the art of observation
That is the labour of the stars' parade.

To him I gave more practical advice
Well grounded in my own experience:
The salary would only just suffice
So don't count on The Board's benevolence!

Within my heart I worried to recall
His coming to a party at Dunsink
In such distress that it was clear to all
His soul that night had hovered on the brink.

I pray to God that he may marry soon
Lest he should end up baying at the moon

Brinkley knew that Boyton was being economical with the truth; he also had a jaundiced view of the College's remuneration. He was the near-witness of Hamilton's suicide attempt, thought to have occurred near the canal bridge that subsequently saw the birth of quaternions.

DR T ROMNEY ROBINSON (Astronomer)

In contrast to my worthy cousin Cloyne
I thought it would be his ideal position:
What wastage if instead he were to join
Those Fellow drudges burdened with tuition.

Besides, I could not see him celibate;
He liked the fairer sex, if over-keen;
A mind like his, so charged and passionate
Would wither on the bough in College Green.

For certain, he was no astronomer,
Less likely to put telescope to eye
Than scan a verse or two of Chapman's Homer;
I offered to acquaint him with the sky

Lest some time in the future none too distant
He's subject to the rule of his assistant!

Romney Robinson, Director of the Armagh Astronomical Observatory, was a strong supporter of Hamilton's application; he knew that Hamilton needed to provide a home for his sisters, which would not have been possible as a Fellow; also the College had recently re-introduced celibacy for Fellows.

CHARLES THOMPSON (Astronomer's Assistant)

I'm left to manage things best as I can
Between the Reverend Doctor's installation
And this new man — hah, more a boy than man
Who scarce could estimate an elevation.

And not a wet week here, he's up and gone
Without a warning, bar a note to say
That I may graze my cow upon his lawn
For now — but not to touch an ounce of hay!

But brains to burn — long evenings at the clár,
His boys and me, in shared incomprehension;
I'd sit awhile and then plead that some star
Now wanted my immediate attention.

Just check the observation log to see
How little there is 'H' compared to 'T'.

When Hamilton was appointed to the Andrews Chair of
Astronomy he became concomitantly Director of Dunsink
Observatory, where he and his family lived. The position
came with an assistant, who probably knew more about
practical astronomy than Hamilton. Hamilton's initial
enthusiasm soon waned, confessing that he had little appetite
for observing. Clár (dubh) is the Irish for blackboard.

ALEXANDER NIMMO (Engineer at large)

Indeed it was a lucky star that brought
Us to Armagh just then; it must be said
I took to him as to a fellow Scot
For all that he was Dublin born and bred.

It wasn't hard to knock him off the track
And let Killarney's Lakes cast their famed spell;
I fear his promise to come swiftly back
Evaporated in my diving bell!

We then proceeded on the morning tide,
Where engineering waits on poetry,
To climb Helvellyn, then to Ambleside
Where Master Wordsworth had us in for tea

And my gross trade was swept into the pan;
Indeed, he truly is an Irishman.

Hamilton accepted Romney Robinson's invitation to improve his observational skills at Armagh Observatory. There he met Nimmo who persuaded him to tour his engineering works in progress in Ireland; the tour extended to England, resulting in the significant introduction to Wordsworth.

WILLIAM WORDSWORTH (Poet)

Of all the would-be poets I have known
— and they would fill the great church of St Paul
Some three or four times over — he alone
Has ill deserved my proffered cup of gall.

That first night walking back to Ambleside,
With none 'except the stars and burning words',
We turned as one, the self same path re-tried
And yet again, like two migrating birds.

Despite the gap in age, we quickly found
Excursion (real and literal) could pace
The solid rock that was our common ground
That "useful knowledge" only can debase.

Affection that could weather any storm
Not least the thorny issue of Reform.

Wordsworth advised Hamilton that he was more likely to achieve fame in mathematics than in poetry; nevertheless, poetry was a significant part of their friendship. An area of agreement was their common dislike of the practical science that would come to dominate the latter part of the century; they held divergent views on political reform.

LADY PAMELA CAMPBELL (Friend)

How fortunate for all that young Adare
Should have him as a tutor and a friend.
We in Armagh were swiftly made aware
Of his poor heart that still refused to mend.

It seems she lived now in our neighbourhood
And he had paid a call, for good or ill,
To find her 'sorrowful', but was it good
That she should visit him on College Hill?

His offer to show her the instrument
Brought them alone together in the dome;
He broke the eyepiece wires in torment.
The lady should have better stayed at home!

I pride myself that my attentive ear
Could bring his anguished soul some little cheer.

Lady Campbell, the daughter of the Irish patriot Lord Edward
Fitzgerald, became Hamilton's confidante in the matter of
Catherine Disney. This was important to Hamilton's wellbeing
following the distressful meeting at Armagh Observatory on
College Hill.

DR HUMPHREY LLOYD (Colleague)

I'd read his tour de force "System of Rays"
But unlike him had missed the satisfaction
Of proving a biaxial displays
The marvel that is conical refraction.

Immediately he's tugging at my sleeve
Demanding that I do the measurement:
These theorists mistakenly believe
That pen and paper makes experiment!

At first my sample of aragonite
Was much too thin for decent separation;
That it was 'macled' added to my plight
But Dollond's crystal saved the situation.

I did it, but it was a close-run thing
With Airy and some others on the wing.

Hamilton announced his prediction on October 22; Lloyd did
not succeed in experimental verification until December 14.
After earlier attempts (macled means crystal twinning) had
failed, Lloyd agreed that Hamilton could offer the opportunity
to Airy. The prediction earned Hamilton the Royal Medal of
the Royal Society and a knighthood.

ELLEN De VERE (Romantic Attachment)

Dear Lord, but what a piece of work's a man,
What theorems and equations say he should
Infer from one remark a whole life's plan
And never ask directly where he stood?

It's true I did say that I could not live
Contentedly apart from Curragh Chase
But could the goose not find the words to give
A girl the chance to row back with good grace?

And as for Dora Wordsworth and her rant
That I was too much wrapped up in my brother?
Her perspicacity was much in want
To write thus to Eliza, as another.

In any case he struck another match
And all may judge who was the better catch!

In later life Ellen indicated to Hamilton's biographer that had
the suit been more vigorously pursued, marriage would have
been acceptable. Hamilton persuaded himself that he admired
Ellen only for her spirituality and taste in poetry; he
subsequently obtained for her Coleridge's autograph.

DEATH

By symmetry you might expect to hear
Three more have shuffled off this mortal coil.
O plenty died, but none that's worth a tear
Or likely to provide reflective foil.

And yet, amid the daily toil and trouble
I almost made my quota of the salt:
To bring off a spectacular, the double
And bring the story to an early halt.

That age-old drama of the star-crossed lovers;
O never was there such a tale of woe …
He came as close as any who discovers
That he is powerless to stop the show.

He held off — God or manners? — from the deep;
This is a pretty pickle that will keep.

PART III

1835 – 1850

Metaphysics

METAPHYSICS

Ta meta ta phusika — from the Greek
And Aristotle's editor's suggestion
That "only post the physicals" I speak;
To be, or not to be, is not the question.

From cradle-rocking to the rolling hearse
Each age has used me for its selfish ends;
From verse potentially to multiverse
I smile upon their urge to make amends.

A third way through this 19th century,
A Europe grown much less militant.
So then, as now, we look to Germany;
A thousand marks to one, it must be Kant,

Whose view of mathematics was to find
The strongest resonance in his pure mind.

Hamilton was introduced to the writings of Kant by the poet and
philosopher, Samuel Taylor Coleridge.

GEORGE TICKNOR (American Literary Scholar)

A Yankee at the court of … now, which king … ?
I guess William the Fourth, a busy man
Who'd fathered ten in an extended fling
With 'Mrs Jordan', Irish courtesan.

I won't detain you with a long narration
Of why I was in Dublin at that time;
The meeting of the new Association
A shining beacon in that city's grime.

Where I was privy to a rare event,
The memory of which will never fade;
Among the Long Room's busts of monument
The Lord Lieutenant laying his sword-blade

Upon the shoulders of your favourite son:
Rise up, Sir William Rowan Hamilton!

Ticknor's is the fullest record of events in the Long Room of
Trinity College, during the meeting of the British Association.
Hamilton was a founder member of the BA and organized its
Dublin meeting in 1835.

SAMUEL TAYLOR COLERIDGE (Poet & Sage)

He had the wisdom and vocabulary
Of someone born decades before his season:
I wrote *Time Real and Imaginary*
When he had barely reached the use of reason.

His Abel, *Reason*, not its Cain–like twin
Of *Understanding*, stood him in good stead;
He knew which one would ultimately win
And turn the Bible story on its head.

Arithmetic derives from intuition
Of time, which words of mine would not gainsay
The mathematics of his erudition
And like The Baptist who prepared the way

I did not witness his re-Kanted rime
That Algebra's the Science of Pure Time.

Wordsworth remarked that Hamilton reminded him more of
Coleridge than any other man he ever met. Hamilton considered
himself a disciple of Coleridge, imbibing his ideas on philosophy,
science and religion.

EDWARD PUSEY (Anglican Theologian)

When Newman set the wolf upon the flock
To bring the 39ers back to Rome
With Canterbury reeling from the shock,
We met at his Observatory home.

For all his talk of Transcendentalism
— Bah, Coleridge! — he hungered after rite
But ill deserved his sister's charge of schism,
Declaring him a "flaming Puseyite".

He told a story how his greyhound *Smoke*
Had chewed upon The Book of Common Prayer.
The beating it received became a joke:
Its name in 'bells and smells' caused it to err!

The exodus that happened in the end
Would see the loss of more than man's best friend.

39ers is a reference to the Thirty Nine Articles of Religion of the Church of England established in 1563. 'The exodus' is the conversion of a number of Hamilton's friends to Roman Catholicism.

JOHN HERSCHEL (Astronomer)

Please do not ask about *The Great Moon Hoax*,
Newspapers will print anything to sell
More copies — though I rather favour jokes
And so did he; I often saw him quell

A flaming row with such at the BA
"the wave men are not wavering … " While I
Took refuge at The Cape, he braved the fray
On undulators — give me the night sky!

He was the heart of our association,
Likewise for many years the stalwart chair
In Dawson Street, a credit to his nation,
As Minstrel Moore would have it: *rich and rare*

And if I had the giving of that boon,
I'd name for him a crater on the moon.

The Great Moon Hoax properly attaches to Herschel's father,
William, also an astronomer; 'undulators' concerned the wave
theory of light, a hotly contested scientific topic of the day. 'BA'
is the British Association and 'Dawson St' the location of the
Royal Irish Academy, of which Hamilton was President for
many years. 'Minstrel Moore' is Tom Moore, songwriter and
poet. There is a lunar crater so named.

VISCOUNT ADARE (Pupil & Friend)

I thank my parents for their great foresight
In placing me a pupil in his care;
No plant in Christendom had better light
Than one that breathed Dunsink's botanic air.

Perhaps too heady, for within short train,
My eyesight weakened by much observation,
My tutor likewise suffering some strain
We're forced to take a well-deserved vacation.

So many journeys hence, yet I still care
About the one that did not go ahead:
When Lloyd resigns, MacCullagh takes that chair
And he then takes MacCullagh's chair instead?

As pro and anti banners were unfurled
He showed quaternions onto the world!

Viscount Adare was Hamilton's introduction to the houses of the
Anglo-Irish aristocracy; he was also a significant promoter of
science and the arts; their friendship was long-lasting, if strained
by Adare's conversion to Roman Catholicism. The Board of
Trinity College was unwilling to sanction Adare's suggestion
regarding the rotation of chairs, largely because Hamilton refused
to take the Fellowship Examination.

LADY HELEN HAMILTON (Spouse)

A Lady, yes, but still without a carriage,
Long treks to Dublin at a walking pace
And there were always three souls in our marriage
Or four, if you count Missy Curragh Chase!

I knew about the whispers behind-backs
That I was just a phantom of a wife,
My absences the focus of attacks;
As if my presence could enlarge his life?

But I was witness to his darker days,
A genius, yes, but still a child half-grown;
I weathered his precocious wants and ways
And gave him three strong children of his own

And I was midwife when, against the odds,
He brought forth his canal-bank set of quads.

In spite of her infirmities and associated absences, Lady
Hamilton remained a central figure in Hamilton's life; his
friends and colleagues were less sympathetic. Humphrey Lloyd
claimed that despite many visits to Dunsink he had never seen
her and T Romney Robinson called her "an abstract idea".
Hamilton discovered quaternions while walking with his wife
along the Royal Canal near Broom (Brougham) Bridge. He
claimed to have scratched the formula $i^2 = j^2 = k^2 = ijk = -1$ on
the wall of the bridge there and then.

JOHN GRAVES (Mathematician)

And nothing in our maths was quite the same:
Quaternions had trampled on our norms,
The commutative law put to the flame
And with it Peacock's *Permanence of Forms*.

I wrote that this new system 'graveled' me
For I too had the triplets much in mind
But I was willing to move on and see
What other fabled treasures we might find.

And which I did, based on the number eight,
His offer to make public gave no hint
That he would manage to procrastinate
Until I had been beaten into print.

And still the thought disturbs too frequent slumbers
My Octaves ever known as Cayley Numbers!

Hamilton had spent 10 years working on triplets before his breakthrough with quaternions. Peacock's Principle required that algebra follow the conventions of arithmetic; quaternions were found to flout the convention that a x b = b x a. John Graves was not the only colleague to suffer from Hamilton's heightened sense of proprietorship.

PROFESSOR JAMES MacCULLAGH (Colleague)

As long as mathematics still shall rule,
The lawyer's son and Talbot's graduate,
The farmer's son and product of hedge school,
They both may enter Trinity's Front Gate.

In reasoning we kept the paths we knew,
His floating with the clouds, my feet of clay;
Small wonder then that as his stature grew,
I claimed to have already passed that way.

In one respect alone I yield the floor:
For all that he appeared the mystic sage
He was the grafter, I the one to pour
My anguished doubts across the empty page.

And so we tip the balance of a life,
The choice between the quill and pocket-knife.

MacCullagh attended a hedge school in rural County Tyrone. *Talbot's* is Talbot's Castle, where Hamilton's Uncle James maintained his school in Trim. Hamilton's concerns about proprietorship derived from claims by MacCullagh that he had anticipated much of Hamilton's discoveries, including conical refraction and quaternions. MacCullagh suffered from depression and cut his own throat in his College rooms.

JAMES WILLIAM BARLOW (Pupil, son of Catherine)

The Founding Chair of Modern History,
Vice Provost, Senior Fellow was my share
And yet the thought has often come to me
That I, perhaps, had better fared elsewhere.

Not only did Mahaffey try to shame
Me with his play on one weak man's reply
To "What is Dr Barlow's claim to fame?"
"I've no idea, Sir!" "Truth, Sir, nor have I!"

But also, when I railed against excess,
They always had a barb to make me smart:
They knew I owed my Fellowship success
To him alone, and to his broken heart.

The Lord shall deal with those quick to condemn.
He was a man the worth of ten of them.

That Hamilton made Barlow his protégé is understandable.
However, it seems less than appropriate that he was
simultaneously tutoring a candidate in a topic (quaternions) for
which he was also supplying questions to the examiners.
Barlow's eventual success in 1848 led to the further (and near-
fatal) re-connection with Catherine. Mahaffey was Provost of
Trinity College.

THOMAS DISNEY (Brother of Catherine)

How merciful that parents should ordain
A daughter's happiness far in advance
Of their own going-off and not remain
To see their handiwork made circumstance.

That is a brother's lot, a sister's care,
And I must answer for misplaced belief
That fifteen years had softened their despair;
Our visit offered neither much relief

Nor later letters, saying I know not
Except they only added to the guilt,
The culmination, one near-fatal tot
Of laudanum, by luck the phial spilt!

And pointless to blame this one or the other.
I leave the last installment to my brother.

Thomas Disney underestimated the persistence of the mutual
attraction between his sister and Hamilton; the visit to Dunsink
was followed by an exchange of letters that was eventually
halted by Catherine's husband; a final letter announcing her
intention to commit suicide reached Hamilton at Parsonstown,
in County Offaly.

WILLIAM PARSONS (Astronomer & Earl of Rosse)

I liked him well enough, though it was clear
Astronomy had no place in his plan:
His visits here, ostensibly to peer
Into the maw of my *Leviathan*,

Would see him wander off, too quickly bored,
To write a verse about us in due course;
I liked the line about the 'wealth free poured'
- as did my wife, whose dowry was the source!

And then there was the time that he received
A letter from a certain lady-friend …
I told my wife, unless I am deceived,
He's headed for a right unhappy end,

Most likely Bedlam, banging on the bars.
You never know what's in another's stars.

Leviathan, a reflecting telescope of 72 inch (1.8 m) aperture, was the largest telescope in the world from 1845 until the construction of the 100 inch (2.5 m) Hooker Telescope in 1917. The telescope was virtually unused for the first three years, because Parsons was occupied in famine relief. Hamilton's poem *Parsonstown Sonnet I* is reproduced on page 91.

GEORGE BIDDELL AIRY (Astronomer Royal)

First, let me make it clear I did *not* lose
To him back then, whatever way it sounds;
Dunsink's a posting I chose to refuse.
For Pity's sake, a mere three hundred pounds?

At Parsonstown, when Rosse proposed champagne
He passed and then again he thought, perhaps
One little glass ... that he was quick to drain;
Old Graves would like to blame *me* for his lapse!

And in his cups he frequently would say
That how I would react to poetry
Would be to make three copies right away
And file them in close order under 'P'.

Well, I can take a drink, and not fall down.
The smartest one can play the greatest clown.

Airy had been a candidate for the Andrews Chair in 1827, and arguably was more deserving of the position. His subsequent distinguished service as Astronomer Royal has been tarnished by allegations that through his inaction, Britain lost the opportunity of priority in the discovery of Neptune. Hamilton's relapse into alcohol abuse was never wholly reversed.

REVEREND ROBERT GRAVES (Friend & Biographer)

I think that I can well and truly say
Two thousand pages and too many years
Will know a man as anybody may.
Forgive me if I tumble into tears

At other linkages we both held dear,
Two brothers of the mathematical
Persuasion and my time in Windermere
As curate to his pards poetical.

No human span is ever free of strife:
His portion brought him often to the brink,
Obsessive love (and faith), an absent wife,
Despair enlarged in alcoholic drink.

Those demons proved to be the heavy load
He carried on his weary earthly road.

Robert Graves' 3-volume work *Life of William Rowan Hamilton* was many years in preparation, finally appearing over the period 1882-89. He was also an important figure in Hamilton's personal life, in particular with regard to curbing the latter's abuse of alcohol.

WILLIAM SMITH O'BRIEN (Friend & Patriot)

I may have met him first down at Adare
A boat trip on the Maigue, we shot the falls:
When I fell in, he leapt without a care
Full-clothéd, and emitting Redskin calls!

Then came respectability and fame;
For all his earlier Reformist zeal
The knighthood and the Castle-keeping game
Meant he would never countenance Repeal.

And after old O'Connell's turn-about
I knew that protest never would suffice,
Young Irelander, I led Kilkenny out
In my intentional blood sacrifice.

And yet, he was among the few that pled
For mercy that I might retain my head.

Smith O'Brien and Hamilton had parted company at the time
of O'Connell's Monster Rallies, with the former moving further
towards militant action; he had earlier caused Hamilton some
embarrassment over a donation to the Royal Irish Academy in
the name of the Repeal Association.

DEATH

A feast or famine? – famine *is* my feast!
Who lives or dies is in the penny's toss.
He kept his head down at his sums; at least
he sought no profit from another's loss.

He coined me five across the River Styx:
First, Cousin Arthur, fountain of goodwill,
Then Boyton, star of College politics
And Uncle James, the lowly curate still.

He mourned these and moved on, as if by rote;
The fourth, though, haunts him like Old Marley's ghost:
The vision of MacCullagh's bloodied throat,
So much alike, affecting him the most

And Wordsworth, in the poet's own words 'bound
Within the sonnet's scanty plot of ground'.

PART IV

1850 – 1865

Poetry

POETRY

From Gilgamesh through Homer to Li Po,
From Chaucer to blind Milton I am proud
To sit and watch my standing army grow,
Yet cast a cold eye on the current crowd.

Whose heart was dancing with the daffodils?
Whose villain of the piece was Ralph The Rover?
Whose gardens that were bright with sinuous rills?
Whose note of sadness on the beach at Dover?

If poetry makes nothing happen might
The other way around be also true?
He countered that when Science bade goodnight
His versifying urge retired too.

He was no Swift, no Donne, nor yet a Pope;
I liked the one about the telescope.

Hamilton begins one letter to Wordsworth with 'As Keats
exclaimed "O for ten years that I may overwhelm myself in
Poesy", so you [Wordsworth] will perhaps exclaim "O for some
Pause that Mr Hamilton may not overwhelm me with his
verses"' He then makes the remark that when he is busiest in
Science, he is likewise in poetry.

AUBREY DE VERE (Poet)

To say the least, I loved him as a brother,
Though there was ample reason for dispute;
His courtship of my sister one such bother,
For I was not in favour of the suit.

It is the measure of him that this fix
Was not enough to put us to the test;
We weathered too the storms of politics
Of Famine and agrarian unrest

But came to grief, as all too frequently,
On that hard rock of true religion's home.
He tithed himself with The Ascendancy
While I made my long journey back to Rome,

To which he would permit just one concession,
Regarding our Church practice of confession.

Hamilton was latterly wearied by De Vere's devotion to the
'Glories of Mary'; De Vere's reputation rests largely on the
religious poetry of this period. The concept of confession
chimed with Hamilton's obsessional need to talk about
Catherine Disney.

DR RICHARD WHATELY (Archbishop)

It should be written in the sacred texts
That Protestant Archbishops have no friends,
Caught in the middle of the warring sects
From Evangelicals to Popish trends.

He was initially one of the first
But then fell under Coleridge's sway
And shortly after found himself immersed
In Newman's Tracts, and almost gone astray.

But age and sense prevailed, in all events
As Warden of the church at Castleknock
He cleansed the place of Roman elements,
The Pelican sent to the butcher's block.

He keeps a painting of The Virgin Mother,
Though some say it's a likeness of another.

As he aged Hamilton became more conservative in politics and
religion; in the latter case he was a devout member of the
Church of Ireland and churchwarden of his parish. Although he
was increasingly critical of those friends who had become
Roman Catholics, he was more embarrassed than enthusiastic
on the issue of the devotional window (complete with pelican
and other Roman Catholic symbols) that had offended
Whately. Hamilton on more than one occasion referred to
'Sancta Catherina".

ROBERT DISNEY (Brother of Catherine)

My sister's health demanded that she keep
Indoors and in our care in Donnybrook;
The cruel harvest that she failed to reap
Had served to bring the principals to book.

But knowing of approaching death she sent
A pencil case inscribed to that effect,
Which roused him so much that I must relent
And let them meet again, in which respect

I granted privacy, brief minutes when
He offered her the book that was his life;
He visited a second time but then
A fortnight on she was beyond all strife.

That evening, I returned to him unread
The letters she had hidden in her bed.

The book was *Lectures on Quaternions.* Hamilton was well aware that the previous correspondence with Catherine was potentially damaging. He burned the originals after copying them out in shorthand into a notebook, labeling it "Neville and Sydney 1850"; on Catherine's death this notebook was returned to Hamilton by Robert Disney.

REV. WILLIAM BARLOW (Husband of Catherine)

Harsh judgement on the sacrament of marriage
If Godly comfort and a goodly ration
Of earthly goods, a home and horse & carriage
Is set at naught by their enduring passion.

How odd it seems that we would never meet?
Though once it happened that he chose to call
Upon my son in rooms; I was discrete
And hid within a doorway in the hall.

But on the very night of my wife's death
I spied him standing in the street below,
The early frost illumining his breath;
His look was the epitome of woe.

May God forgive my thinking that our plights
Were borrowed from that trashy *Wuthering Heights.*

Hamilton believed he was justified in his hatred of Reverend Barlow. However, it would seem that the latter was the injured party. In his person he appears to have been a caring pastor, active in Famine Relief and showing bravery in times of rural unrest.

DR ANDREW HART (College Bursar)

We had, of course, been down this road before:
His *Lectures on Quaternions* had run
To seven hundred pages, and who bore
The cost, when sales in Dublin numbered none?

A shorter simple manual, said his peers,
The length to be contained within strict bounds.
He promised to deliver in two years;
We voted him a cautious hundred pounds.

But four years on, *The Elements* outgrew
The Lectures and the manual was portrayed
As reference book, no finish yet in view
And here's the printer wanting to be paid.

He quoted Xenophon with nonchalance:
Ten Thousand were his hours in advance!

Xenophon wrote about the 10,000 strong army of Greek soldiers. After Hamilton's death The Board of Trinity College covered the outstanding costs of publication of *Elements of Quaternions*, amounting to £500. Hamilton's estate retained copyright but the College acquired Hamilton's papers; it also funded the monumental 3-part *Life of William Rowan Hamilton*, authored by Robert Percival Graves.

LADY JANE FRANCESCA WILDE (Poet)

Speranza was my pen name at *The Nation;*
And when they read my call to armed aggression
Poor Gavan Duffy faced incarceration,
The court unwilling to heed *my* confession.

But that was some six years before we met;
My husband knew him — after we had dined
I asked him to be sponsor when we'd wet
Our little pagan's head but he declined.

'A Feast of Poets' held in '58
On Shakespeare's birthday, April 23rd,
We gathered at Dunsink to celebrate
In laughter, music and in spoken word.

Although he was an out-and-out High Tory
He laboured, like us all, for Ireland's Glory.

The court chose to disbelieve Lady Wilde's claim of authorship of the offending article. The 'little pagan' was the celebrated Oscar.

JOHN JAQUES (Toy Manufacturer)

Gold Medal Winner at the '51
Great Exhibition for the novel game
Of *Croquet*, and 'the empire where the sun
Shall never set' spread far and wide its fame.

I'd seen a version in The Emerald Isle
And its success had made me more inclined
To think his strange Icosian would while
Away an hour in 'crookey' of the mind.

He was ecstatic with my cheque, the same
Could not be said for me. So, what went wrong?
Perhaps they balked at its tongue-twister name
Compared with *Snap* or *Ludo* or *Ping Pong*.

The truth was yet another box of tricks;
It proved too easy for a child of six!

John Jaques did not recoup his investment in The Icosian Game. He also had to dissuade Hamilton from including a lengthy explanation of icosian calculus in the instructions.

MICHAEL HENRY GILL (Printer)

The Annals of The Four Masters had run
To seven volumes with new Gaelic type
And Hincks's Eastern scripts were timely done,
Plus plenty more, without a single gripe.

The Lectures were a challenge but we stayed
On good terms, such that he could joke I knew
My beta from my theta and not shade
Its import any less than p from q.

But with *The Elements* the workload soared
Like Dodgson's *Alice* it just grew and grew;
I had to go directly to The Board,
A fracture unrepaired by printers' glue.

And it provided little vindication
To see him buried ere its publication.

Shortly after the publication of *Lectures on Quaternions*, Michael Gill branched out into the publishing and bookselling business. Gill & Macmillan is an established publisher of books in Ireland today.

WILLIAM EDWIN HAMILTON (Son)

When my poor father yielded to the gout
I had to cope with no small heap of pother,
A mother ill, a sister's health in doubt
So that she must be lodging with my brother.

It also fell to me the final task
Of readying his book for publication;
I should have used that moment to unmask
The hypocrites of this ungrateful nation.

For while he laboured on it day and night,
Why, even as he lay on his deathbed,
His creditors, unsparing of his plight
Were heaping further coals upon his head.

A fortnight on, I once again took ship
And bade farewell for good to this sad kip!

After college William trained as an engineer, at great expense to
his father. Together with his Aunt Sydney he joined a scam
expedition to South America, adding further to that expense.
He settled in Canada, where after involvement in get-rich
schemes, all of which ended in failure, he was a smalltime
publisher.

REVEREND ARCHIBALD HAMILTON (Son)

By now, of course, it is the stuff of fable,
A childhood fancy that we can't forget;
Our daily greeting at the breakfast table:
Can Papa multiply the triplets yet?

He was a loving father, and at times
Much more, our mother often indisposed,
A font of clever puzzles and fun rhymes
That he, most like, had instantly composed.

And anxious for our futures — if I may
Speak of my brother's so-called expertise?
My father borrowed what he scarce could pay
To fund those wild schemes in the colonies.

While I, like him, kept to our native sod
And put my trust in Ireland, and my God.

'Arch' was a most unconventional clergyman, who quarreled with
his church superiors. He also invested (and lost) money in his
brother's schemes. His relatives thought him somewhat deranged.
In old age he loved to tell children the stories of Old Ireland.

HELEN ELIZA O'REGAN (Daughter)

From early age his name for me was *Moo*
The why of that is well and truly gone
But possibly — which is my brothers' view —
It's from Old Thompson's cow that grazed our lawn.

He kept the most engaging range of friends
Across the spectrum, Science and The Arts,
The postman bribed to wait while he amends
His letters to those far flung foreign parts.

And by return would come their long replies,
Mysterious De Morgan's quick *bon mot*,
Miss Edgeworth's stories to delight our eyes
— I'm writing too, a novel, but it's slow.

I'm sorry that he did not live to see
My marriage of such perfect harmony.

Graves describes Helen as "sweet, bright, shy and rather
eccentric". She married her father's friend Archdeacon John
O'Regan, 23 years her senior. She died of complications after
the birth of their son, John R H O'Regan; the novel was
unfinished.

PROFESSOR PETER GUTHRIE TAIT (Mathematician)

Why, yes, I do suppose I was 'the rock'!
His first disciple, loyal to the end;
When others gathered round to jeer and mock,
Mine was the unsheathed sword raised to defend,

An effort that was never well repaid.
His to-and-fro would make an angel vexed;
My own book of examples was delayed
While he rebuilt Mount Tabor out of text.

The 'vector' men laid siege to that high peak;
So many self-proclaimed Hyperions
Who sneered quaternions were the unique
And natural way to treat … quaternions?

In times to come, I barrack each poltroon,
Quaternions will take us to the moon!

Tait was an active exponent of quaternion algebra during
Hamilton's life and subsequently. He quarreled publicly with
Heaviside, the originator of the putdown remark about the value
of quaternions. Quaternions are used to plot space travel.

EAMON DE VALERA (Rebel & Politician)

To love one's country is no easy task
To love one's mathematics no less so;
Who was the wag that was the first to ask
How come 6 into 26 won't go?

When I was serving time in Lincoln Jail
Our prison journal ran a competition
On 'My Best Girl'; my poem chose to hail
Quaternia, the queen of demolition!

In keeping with his brand of exegesis
My Institute's strange fellows shared one bed
Where Celtic Gods encounter High Mathesis
With Erwin Schrödinger as its first head.

Teach Hamilton a refuge for the sage
As Ireland takes her place on the world stage.

De Valera was a keen mathematician. His poem ends with the
lines "Shall thou and I beloved, find the means / to knock
Algebra into smithereens". '6 into 26 won't go' refers to the
partition of 32-county Ireland. De Valera's poem 'My Best Girl'
is reproduced on page 92.

ERWIN SCHRÖDINGER (Mathematical Physicist)

Teach Hamilton — our happiest of days
Among a people wonderfully odd,
As when O'Nolan linked our first forays
To write of "Two St Patricks and no God!"

He is, perhaps, the ghost in the machine
Of Quantum Physics, with his clanking chain
Announcing the analogy between
Mechanics and optics; first to distain

Commutativity; re-formulation
Of energy in systems large and small;
He is the "H" in Schrödinger's Equation
And hence the Doktorvater of us all.

Teach Hamilton? As well the stars above
Unless, perhaps, in Elements of Love.

The word *teach* in Irish means house, with macaronic confusion
when a another Hamilton came to the Institute to give a lecture.
O'Nolan's "Two St Patricks and no God!" jibe in *The Irish Times*
conflated Schrödinger's lecture on 'Causality' with Professor
O'Rahilly's address on 'Paladius and Patrick'. It is likely that
Hamilton would have been scandalized by (if also somewhat
envious of) Schrödinger's extra-marital affairs.

DEATH

Eliza is the first to meet Her Maker,
To willingly embark on Charon's boat;
For all of Wordsworth's care she found no taker
Of any of the "rugged" verse she wrote.

Then Catherine, who'd lingered overlong
As if in mirror of the preparation
Of *Lectures on Quaternions*, her song
Is sung, the stage in empty desolation.

And so our hero takes his final bow;
He has cranked out his ultimate full rhyme;
No tug of Uncle's string will wake him now;
He has exhausted his share of pure time.

For fool or savant, commoner or knight
No one evades the dying of the light.

Uncle James's method of waking up his young nephew was to
tie a string to the bedclothes, the string fed through a hole in
the wall of their adjoining bedrooms. Hamilton died peacefully
at home, surrounded by his family.

PARSONSTOWN SONNET I

(Composed in the Upper Gallery of the Great Telescope)

I stood expecting, in the Gallery,
On which shine down the Heaven's unnumbered eyes,
Poised in mid air by art and labour wise,
When with mind's toil mechanic skill did vie,
And wealth free poured, to build that structure high,
Castle of Science, where a Rosse might raise
(His enterprise achieved of many days)
To clustering worlds aloft the Tube's bright Eye.
Pursuing still its old Homeric march,
Northward beneath the Pole slow wheeled the Bear;
Rose over head the great Galactic Arch;
Eastward the Pleiads with their tangled hair;
Gleamed to the west, far seen, the Lake below;
And through the trees was heard the River's flow.

— *William Rowan Hamilton*

Appendix 2

MY BEST GIRL

When I behold thee filled am I with hope
                          Quaternia
And realms new yield my soul extended scope
                          Quaternia
Rich fruit of thought rise to a height divine
When thou I see and know that thou are mine
                          Quaternia
Long through The Ages have our twin souls sped
                          Quaternia
Each on a path which towards its mate was led
                          Quaternia
Till through the spaces infinite thou came
Thy thrilling soul call unto me like flame
                          Quaternia
Until at last our spirits came to rest
                          Quaternia
And I beloved found thee and was blest
                          Quaternia
And in the ages yet to rise and roll
Until anhiliation's awful knell shall toll
Shall thou and I beloved find the means
To knock Algebra into smithereens
                          Quaternia.

— *Eamon de Valera*